♡ a tiny manifesto ♡

operating systems are

AWESOME

the strace zine thinks:

♡ your computer is yours

♡ your OS is yours

♡ open licenses mean you can
READ AND CHANGE THE CODE!!

♡ Linux is REALLY COOL

-›-›-›-›-›-›-›-›-›-›-›-›-›-›-›-›-›-›-›yaaaaay -›-›-›-›-›-›-›-›

LET'S GO LEARN

-›-›-›-›-›-›-›-›-›-›-›-›-›-›-›-›→ →→-›-›→ it's

what is this strace thing?

on OSX
you can use
dtrace/dtruss

pronounced
↙ ess-trace

{strace} is a program on Linux that
lets you inspect what a program is
doing without:

- a debugger
- or the source code
- or even knowing the programming language
  at all (?!??! how can it be?)

Basically strace makes you a wizard ☺

strace! what config file
does bash open when
it starts?

.bashrc!

strace

thank you!

To understand how this works, let's talk a
little about {operating systems} !

Why you should ♡ your
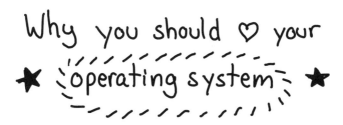
★ operating system ★

Some things it does for you:

- understands how your hard drive works and how the file system on it organizes the bytes into files so you can just read the file

- runs code everytime you press a key so that you can type

- implements networking protocols like TCP/IP so that you can get ~~webpages~~ pictures of cats from the internet

- keeps track of all the memory every process is using

- basicallly knows everything about how all your hardware works so you can just write programs ♡

but wait, Julia, how do my programs use all this great stuff the operating system does?

you

amazing!

SYSTEM CALLS!!!

yay!

wow!

julia

System calls are <u>the API for your operating system</u>:

want to open a file? use `open` and then `read` and `write` to it

sending data over a network? Use `connect` to open a connection and `send` and `recv` pictures of cats.

really, all of them!

<u>Every</u> program on your computer is using system calls <u>all the time</u> to manage memory, write files, do networking, and lots more.

a first cup of strace

You might think with all the talk of operating systems and system calls that using strace is hard.

Getting started is easy! If you have a Linux machine, I want you to try it RIGHT NOW.

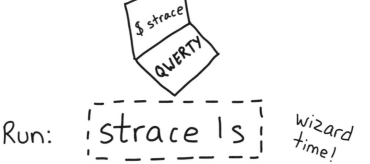

Run: ` strace ls `   wizard time!

There's a LOT of output and it's pretty confusing at first. I've annotated some for you on the next page. ☺

try stracing more programs! Google the system calls! Don't worry if you don't understand everything! I sure don't.

annotated strace

When you run strace, you'll see thousands of lines of output like this:

```
$ strace ls /home/bork/blah
execve("/bin/ls", ["ls", "/home/bork/blah"], [/* 62 vars
*/]) = 0
brk(NULL)                               = 0xb67000
open("/etc/ld.so.cache", O_RDONLY|O_CLOEXEC) = 3
open("/proc/filesystems", O_RDONLY)     = 3
 ... omitted ...
open("/home/bork/blah", O_RDONLY|O_NONBLOCK|O_DIRECTORY) =
3
fstat(3, {st_mode=S_IFDIR|0775, st_size=168, ...}) = 0
getdents(3, /* 3 entries */, 32768)     = 80
getdents(3, /* 0 entries */, 32768)     = 0
close(3)                                = 0
fstat(1, {st_mode=S_IFCHR|0620, st_rdev=makedev(136,
5), ...}) = 0
write(1, "awesome_file\n", 13)          = 13
close(1)                                = 0
close(2)                                = 0
exit_group(0)                           = ?
```

Studies show this is not self-explanatory
(me asking my friends if it makes sense and NOPE NOPE)

★ let's learn how to interpret strace output ★

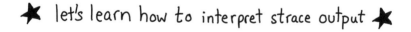

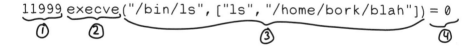

① The process ID (included when you run strace -f)
② The name of the system call (execve starts programs 💀)
③ The system call's arguments, in this case a program to
   start and the arguments to start it with
④ The return value

Here's an example of how to interpret an open system call (opening a file!) in a little more depth:

system call name → | file to open → | open with read/write permissions → | file descriptor

open("awesome.txt", O_RDWR) = 3

The 3 here is a file descriptor number. Internally, Linux tracks open files with numbers! You can see all the file descriptors for process ID 42 and what they point to by doing:

fd is for file descriptor!

```
$ ls -l /proc/42/fd
```

and here's what strace displays when a program reads from a file:

file descriptor ↓ | what got read ↓ | number of bytes read

read(3, "wow! yay!") = 9

If you don't understand something in your strace output:

★ it's normal! There are lots of system calls and
★ it's ok if you don't know what futex does yet
try reading the man page for the system call!

```
$ man 2 open
```

★ remember that just understanding
read + write + open + execve
can take you a long way

my fav♡rite system calls

open

Have you ever not been sure what configuration files a program is using? THAT NEVER NEEDS TO HAPPEN TO YOU AGAIN 🙂🙂🙂. Skip the docs and head straight for:

```
$ strace -f -e open mplayer
       never-gonna-give-you-up.mp3
```

> checking what files a program is opening is my #1 favorite thing to do with strace ♡

write

Programs write logs.

If you're sure your program is writing Very Important Information but don't know what or where, `strace -e write` may be for you.

`read` is super useful too!

connect

Sometimes a program is sending network requests to another machine and I want to know WHICH MACHINE.

```
$ strace -e connect PROGRAM
```

shows me every IP address a program connects to.

Sendto + recvfrom

What's fun? Spying on network activity is fun. If you have a HTTP service and you're debugging and totally at your wits' end, maybe it's time to look at what's REALLY EXACTLY being sent over the network...

these are your pals ♡

execve

Once on my first day of work, a Ruby script that ran some ssh commands wasn't working. Oh no!
But who wants to read the code to find out why? Neither of us did.

```
$ strace -f -e execve ./script.rb
```

told us what the problem ssh command was, and we fixed it!

strace command line flags I ♡

Overwhelmed by all the system calls you don't understand? Try

$ strace -e open

and it'll just show you open system calls. much simpler. ♥

is for follow

Does your program start subprocesses?

Use -f to see what those are doing too. Or just always use -f! That's what I do.

is for PID

"OH NO! I STARTED THE PROGRAM 6 HOURS AGO AND NOW I WAnnT TO STRACE IT!"

don't worry! Just find your program's PID (like 747) and run:

tip: if the process runs as root, you'll need to be root, too because SECURITY

$ strace -p 747

-s is for strings!!

Sometimes I'm looking at the output of a recvfrom and it's like:

recvfrom(6, "and then the monster...")
and OH NO THE SUSPENSE.

strace -s 800 will show you the first 800 characters oof each string. I use -s all the time.

-o is for output!

Let's get real. No matter what, strace prints way too much output. Use:

```
$ strace -o too_much_stuff.txt
```

and sort through it later.

-y

Have no idea which file the file descriptor "3" refers to? -y is a flag in newer versions of strace, and it'll show you filenames instead of just numbers! -yy does the same for sockets too.

Putting it all together:

Want to spy on a ssh session?

```
$ strace -f -o ssh.txt ssh juliabox.com
```

Want to see what files a Dropbox sync process (with PID 230) is opening?

```
$ strace -f -p 230 -e open
```

That's it! Now you're a

☆ WIZARD ☆

More seriously, there's obviously a TON more to learn about operating systems and many further levels of wizardry. But I find just strace by itself to be an incredibly useful tool.

And so fun! On a 12-hour train ride from New York to Montreal, I had no book and no internet.
So I just started stracing programs on my computer, and I could totally figure out how the `killall` program works without reading the source code or ANYTHING.

I learned about strace 5 years ago and even though I know about lots more tools though it's often still the first thing I reach for.

★ happy stracing ★